AUG 11 2008

AUG 28 2008
NOV 03 2008
JAN 13 2009
FEB 25 2009

Withdrawn

MAY 14 2009
JUN 18 2009
JUL 15 2009
AUG 07 2009
OCT 09 2009

MAR 31

Northville District Library
212 W. Cady Street
Northville, MI 48167-1560

P9-CSU-295

Bugs, Bugs, Bugs!

Mosquitoes

by Margaret Hall

Consulting Editor: Gail Saunders-Smith, PhD

Consultant: Laura Jesse, Extension Associate
Department of Entomology
Iowa State University
Ames, Iowa

Capstone press

Mankato, Minnesota

Pebble Plus is published by Capstone Press,
151 Good Counsel Drive, P.O. Box 669, Mankato, Minnesota 56002.
www.capstonepress.com

Copyright © 2006 by Capstone Press. All rights reserved.
No part of this publication may be reproduced in whole or in part, or stored in a retrieval system, or transmitted in any form or by any means, electronic, mechanical, photocopying, recording, or otherwise, without written permission of the publisher. For information regarding permission, write to Capstone Press, 151 Good Counsel Drive, P.O. Box 669, Dept. R, Mankato, Minnesota 56002.
Printed in the United States of America

1 2 3 4 5 6 11 10 09 08 07 06

Library of Congress Cataloging-in-Publication Data
Hall, Margaret, 1947–
Mosquitoes / by Margaret Hall.
p. cm.—(Pebble Plus. Bugs, bugs, bugs!)
Summary: "Simple text and photographs present mosquitoes, how they look, and what they do"—Provided by publisher.
Includes bibliographical references and index.
ISBN-13: 978-0-7368-5351-4 (hardcover)
ISBN-10: 0-7368-5351-0 (hardcover)
1. Mosquitoes—Juvenile literature. I. Title. II. Pebble plus. Bugs, bugs, bugs!
QL536.H34 2006
595.772—dc22   2005023791

Editorial Credits
Mari C. Schuh, editor; Linda Clavel, set designer; Kia Adams, book designer; Jo Miller, photo researcher; Scott Thoms, photo editor

Photo Credits
Bill Johnson, 13
Bruce Coleman Inc., Bartomeu Borrell, 6–7; Kerry T. Givens, 15
Corbis/PHIL/CDC, 1
Dwight R. Kuhn, cover, 11, 17
Getty Images Inc./New Orleans Mosquito and Termite Control Board/Jack Leonard, 9
Photo Researchers Inc./Darwin Dale, 21; Nature's Images/David M. Schleser, 18–19; Nature Source/USDA, 5
USDA/ARS, back cover

Note to Parents and Teachers

The Bugs, Bugs, Bugs! set supports national science standards related to the diversity of life and heredity. This book describes and illustrates mosquitoes. The images support early readers in understanding the text. The repetition of words and phrases helps early readers learn new words. This book also introduces early readers to subject-specific vocabulary words, which are defined in the Glossary section. Early readers may need assistance to read some words and to use the Table of Contents, Glossary, Read More, Internet Sites, and Index sections of the book.

3 9082 10867 0111

JUN 2 4 2008

Northville District Library
212 West Cady Street
Northville MI 48167

Table of Contents

What Are Mosquitoes?

Mosquitoes are small insects with long, thin legs.

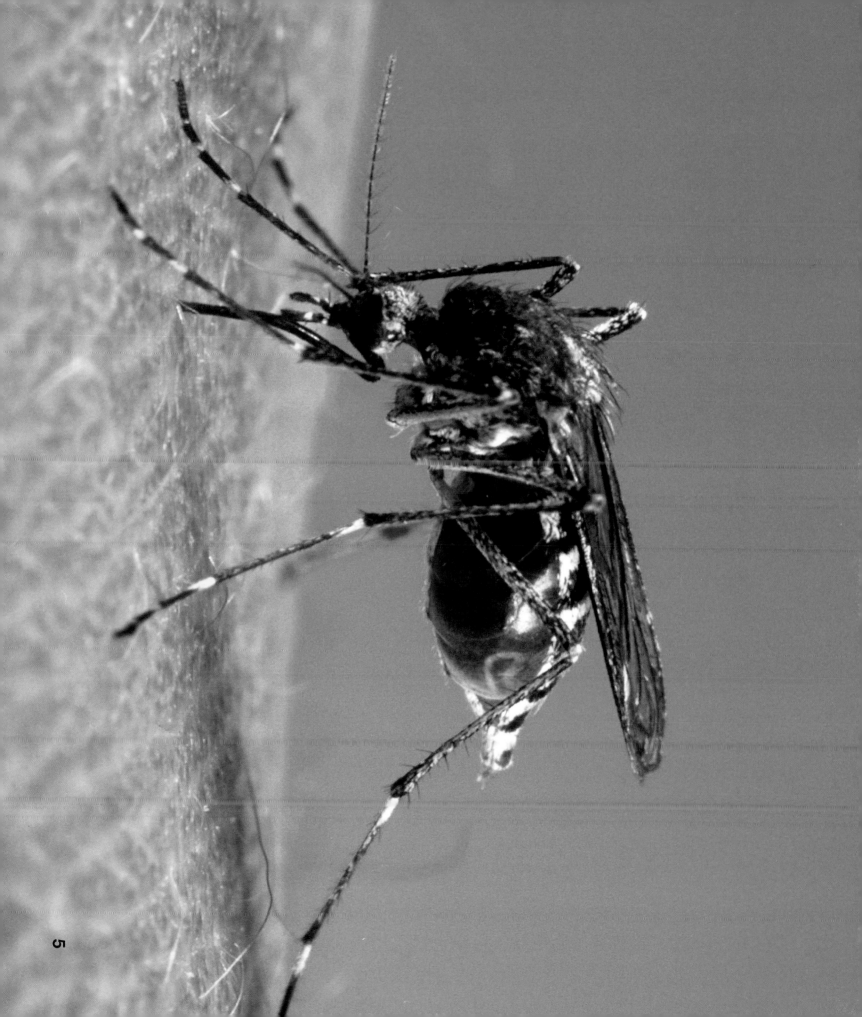

How Mosquitoes Look

Most mosquito bodies
are about the size
of a grain of rice.

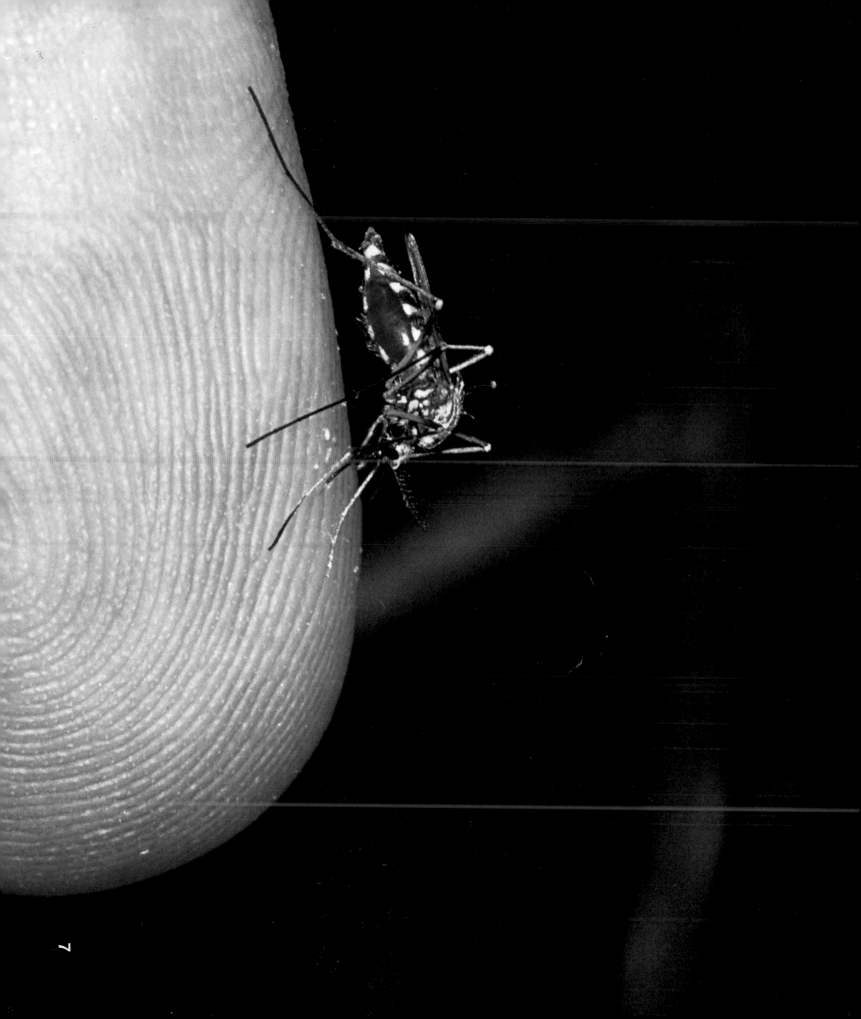

Mosquitoes are black,
gray, or brown.
Some mosquitoes
have white stripes.

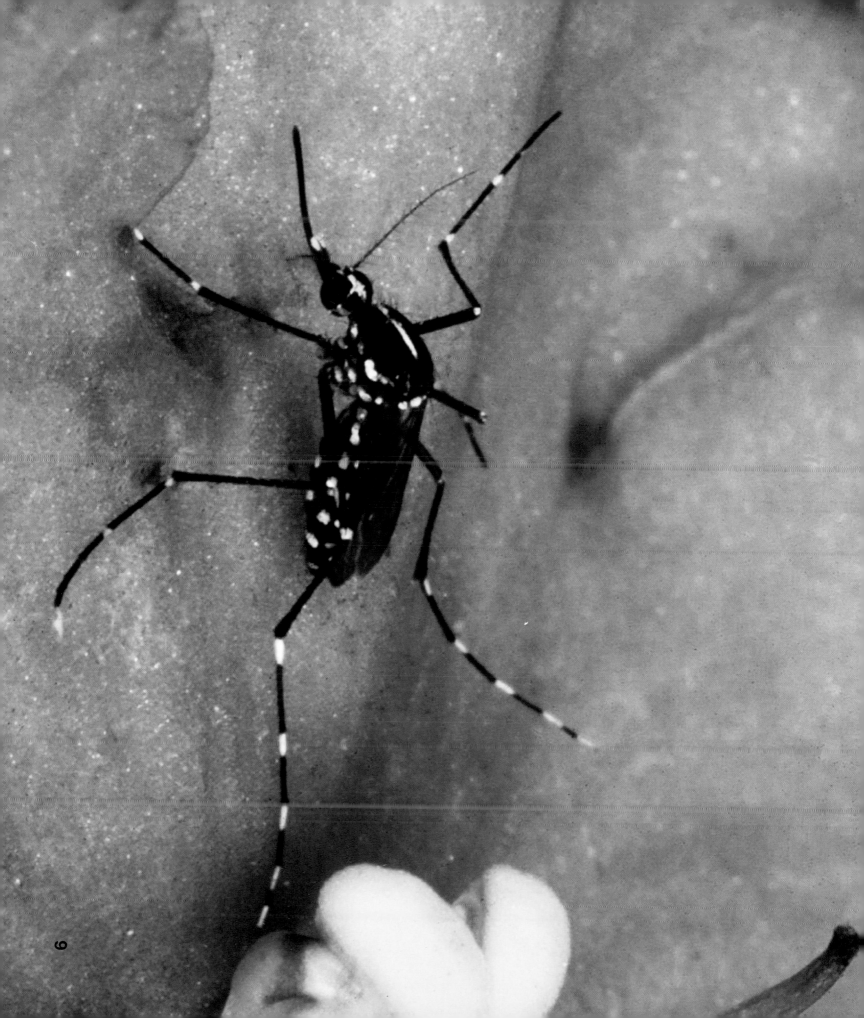

6

Mosquitoes have
two thin wings.
Their wings
make a buzzing noise.

11

Mosquitoes have
curved mouthparts.
The middle is shaped
like a needle.

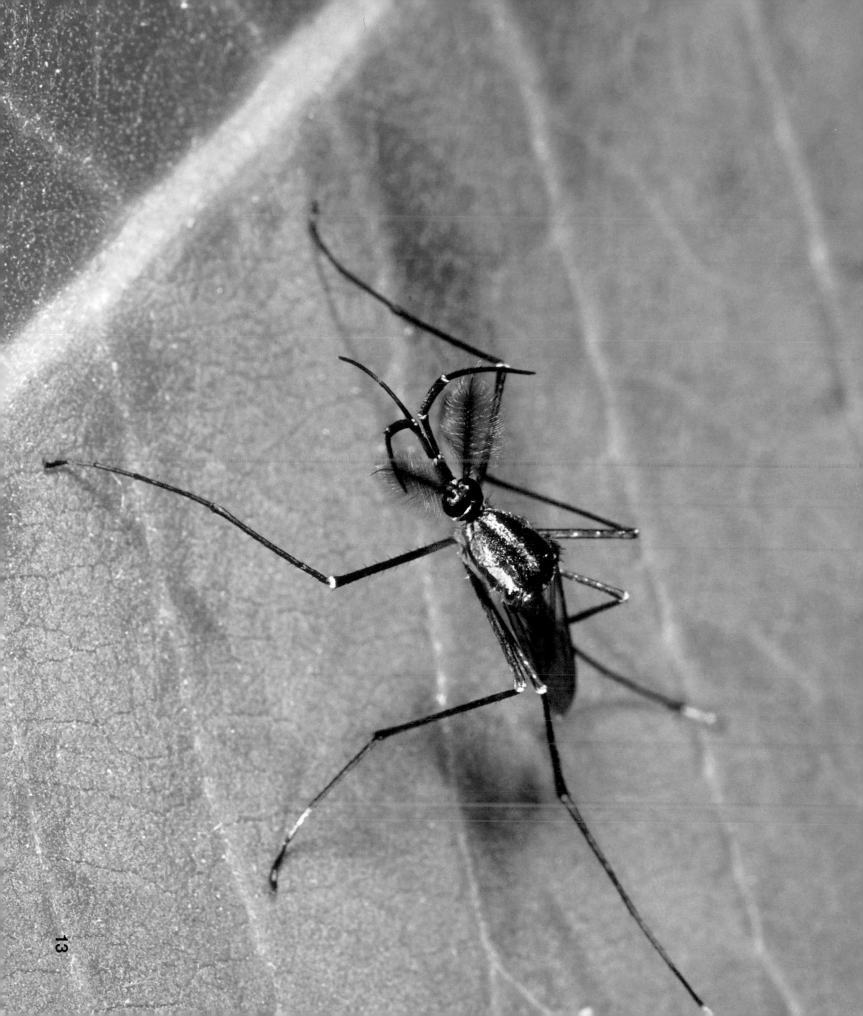

13

What Mosquitoes Do

Mosquitoes stick

their mouthparts into flowers.

They drink nectar

from the flowers.

Female mosquitoes
bite and suck blood.
Females need blood to help
them make eggs.

Female mosquitoes sometimes lay their eggs in muddy ponds. Eggs hatch in a few days in warm weather.

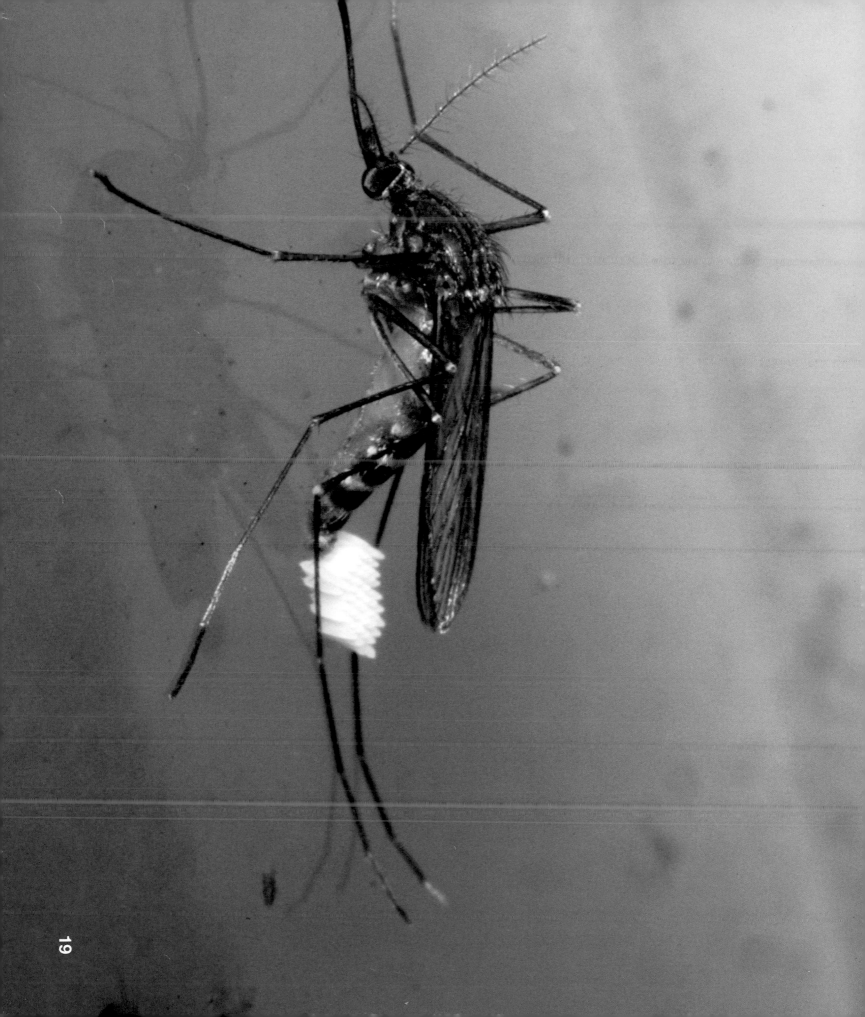

After hatching,
mosquitoes become adults
in just a few days.
They wait for their wings to dry.
Then they fly away.

Glossary

bite—to hurt skin by using teeth, stingers, or mouthparts; when mosquitoes bite, they can sometimes make people and animals sick.

female—an animal that can give birth to young animals or lay eggs

hatch—to break out of an egg

insect—a small animal with six legs, three body sections, and two antennas; most insects have wings and can fly.

nectar—a sweet liquid in flowers that some insects collect and eat as food

Read More

Jacobs, Liza. *Mosquitoes. Wild Wild World.* San Diego: Blackbirch Press, 2003.

Kalman, Bobbie. *The Life Cycle of a Mosquito. The Life Cycle Series.* New York: Crabtree, 2004.

Miller, Heather. *Mosquito. Bugs.* San Diego: Kidhaven Press, 2004.

Murray, Julie. *Mosquitoes. Animal Kingdom.* Edina, Minn.: Abdo, 2003.

Internet Sites

FactHound offers a safe, fun way to find Internet sites related to this book. All of the sites on FactHound have been researched by our staff.

Here's how:

1. Visit www.facthound.com

2. Type in this special code **0736853510** for age-appropriate sites. Or enter a search word related to this book for a more general search.

3. Click on the **Fetch It** button.

FactHound will fetch the best sites for you!

Index

Word Count: 118
Grade: 1
Early-Intervention Level: 14